D1250828

# What's So Great About . . . ?

# AMELIA EARHART

Amie Jane Leavitt

Mitchell Lane
PUBLISHERS

P.O. Box 196
Hockessin, Delaware 19707
Visit us on the web: www.mitchelllane.com
Comments? email us: mitchelllane@mitchelllane.com

249 2946

# *Mitchell Lane* PUBLISHERS

Printing       1        2        3        4        5        6        7        8        9

### A Robbie Reader/What's So Great About . . . ?

| | | |
|---|---|---|
| **Amelia Earhart** | Anne Frank | Annie Oakley |
| Christopher Columbus | Daniel Boone | Davy Crockett |
| Elizabeth Blackwell | Ferdinand Magellan | Francis Scott Key |
| Galileo | George Washington Carver | Harriet Tubman |
| Helen Keller | Henry Hudson | Jacques Cartier |
| Johnny Appleseed | Paul Bunyan | Robert Fulton |
| Rosa Parks | Sam Houston | |

Library of Congress Cataloging-in-Publication Data
Leavitt, Amie Jane.
    Amelia Earhart / by Amie Jane Leavitt.
        p. cm. — (A Robbie Reader. what's so great about—?)
    Includes bibliographical references and index.
    ISBN-13: 978-1-58415-576-8 (library bound)
    1. Earhart, Amelia, 1897–1937—Juvenile literature. 2. Air pilots—United States—Biography—Juvenile literature. 3. Women air pilots—United States—Biography—Juvenile literature. I. Title.
TL540.E3L42 2008
629.13092—dc22
[B]
                                                                                    2007000804

**ABOUT THE AUTHOR:** Amie Jane Leavitt is the author of numerous articles, puzzles, workbooks, and tests for kids and teens. Ms. Leavitt is a former teacher who has taught all subjects and grade levels. She loves to travel, play tennis, and learn new things every day as she writes. She, too, believes in following your dreams.

**PHOTO CREDITS:** Cover, p. 18—Getty Images; pp. 1, 3—NASA; pp. 4, 8, 10—FPG/Getty Images; p. 12—Stephen Pitcairn; p. 16—Keystone/Hulton Archive/Getty Images; p. 19—New York Times Co./Getty Images; pp. 20, 24—Library of Congress; p. 25—Jonathan Scott.

                                                                                    PPC

# TABLE OF CONTENTS

Words in **bold** type can be found in the glossary.

Amelia Earhart took her first plane ride in December 1920. She later remembered, "By the time I got two or three feet off the ground, I knew I had to fly." Two weeks later, she took her first flying lesson.

# A Perfect Day for Flying

It was a warm day in Southern California. The sky was as blue as a robin's egg and the clouds were as soft as cotton. It was a perfect day for flying.

A group of people stood on an airfield looking at the sky. They cheered when two planes zipped through the clouds. They clapped when the planes made loops in the air.

The year was 1920. Airplanes were new to the world. Many in the crowd were watching planes fly for the first time. Twenty-three-year-old Amelia Earhart (AIR-hart) was one of them.

Amelia smiled as she watched the planes do their tricks. She tapped her father on the shoulder. "I think I'd like to fly," she said.

Amelia Earhart lived during a time when few women had careers. About this, she said, "Women must try to do things as men have tried. When they fail, their failure must be but a challenge to others."

Edwin Earhart wanted his daughter to try new things. He could tell this was important to her. He talked to one of the pilots after the show. The man said he would take her in his plane the next day.

Amelia was so excited, she had a hard time sleeping that night. All she could think about was flying.

The next day they went to the field early. Amelia sat in the front seat of the plane. The pilot started the engine and hopped in the back. He **taxied** (TAK-seed) down the dirt road and moved the controls. The plane lifted into the air. They were flying.

The world looked different from the sky. Buildings were smaller. Fields looked like long green rectangles. Amelia felt like a bird. Before the plane landed, she made up her mind. She would be a pilot.

7

Amelia (right) and her sister, Muriel, in 1900. Muriel once said: "Amelia was a person who wanted things accomplished. She was interested in so many things—flying, horses, poetry, sports, reading—almost everything. . . . She was filled with curiosity [kyur-ee-AH-sih-tee] and a sense of adventure."

# Old Wood and Rusty Wire

Amelia Earhart was born on July 24, 1897, in Atchison (AA-chih-sun), Kansas. She was the first child of Edwin and Amy Earhart. She had a younger sister named Muriel (MYOOR-ee-ul).

Edwin was a lawyer who worked for the railroad. Amy stayed home to raise the children. Before she was married, Amy liked to try difficult things. She was the first woman to climb Pike's Peak, a tall mountain in Colorado. She was very brave.

Life was different for children in the 1900s than it is today. Most girls were not allowed to play sports. They were expected to wear dresses and play with dolls. Amelia was lucky because her mother and father didn't think this

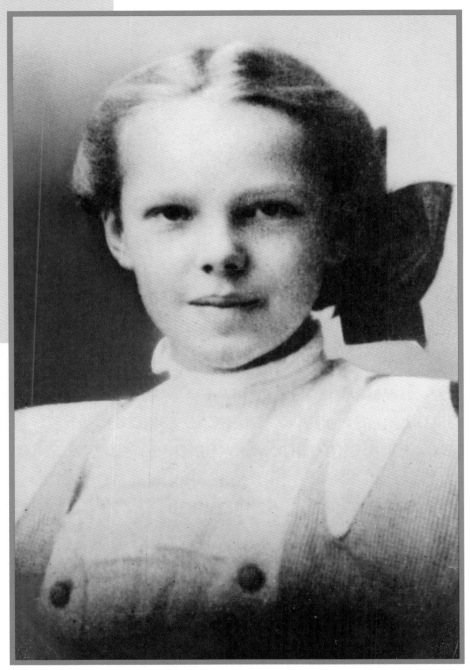

As a young girl, Amelia was known to her friends as AE. This photo of her was taken in 1904, when she was seven years old.

way. They knew girls could do anything boys could do.

Amelia loved fishing with her father and climbing trees in her yard. She liked saving bugs in jars and finding frogs. She also liked to build things. One summer she built her own roller coaster. Amelia would climb in the small wooden seat and speed down the track like a rocket. She said it felt just like flying.

Edwin Earhart took his family on many trips. When Amelia was only ten years old, the family went to a state fair. This is when she saw her first airplane—although it wasn't flying. She didn't think too much of this new machine. To her it just looked like splintery old wood and rusty wire.

Like all kids, Amelia felt lonely at times. Her family moved often because of her father's job. It was hard for her to make friends when she was always the new kid. But Amelia still worked hard and got good grades. After high school, she went on to **college** (KAH-lidj).

11

Amelia sits with her feet in the cockpit of a Pitcairn PCA-2 Autogiro (AW-toh-jy-roh). An autogiro is like a helicopter with airplane wings. In 1931, Amelia flew one of these aircraft to set a world **altitude** (AL-tih-tood) record of 18,415 feet (5,613 meters).

# A Plane as Yellow as a Sunflower

Amelia kept trying new things her whole life. She took fun classes in college. She even learned how to fix car engines.

For Christmas 1917, she went to visit her sister in Canada. She saw soldiers who had been hurt in World War I, and she decided to become a nurse to help them. Later, Amelia went back to college and took classes in medicine. She thought about becoming a doctor.

Few women at this time were like Amelia. Most women married young and stayed home to take care of their children. They didn't have

Before Amelia became a pilot, she had many other types of jobs. During World War I, she was a nurse's aid in Toronto, Canada. She worked in Toronto's Spadina Military Hospital.

**careers** (kuh-REERS). Amelia didn't want this kind of life. She wanted something different.

In 1920, Amelia moved to California. She lived with her parents in Los Angeles (los AN-jeh-lus). She liked the area. It was exciting and new. It seemed like everyone there looked forward to the future and wanted to try new things.

Flying was very popular in California. In fact, this is where Amelia saw her first air show and decided to become a pilot.

Neta Snook was a famous female aviator. She taught Amelia, and many other women, how to fly.

Amelia took flying lessons from a woman pilot named Neta Snook (snuk). It cost a lot of money to become a pilot. She took a part-time job at a telephone company to pay for her lessons. Her parents gave her some money to help buy her first plane. It was small and fast and as yellow as a sunflower. She named it the *Canary* (kuh-NAYR-ee).

Amelia took lessons for six months, until she knew enough about flying to go up on her own. She was finally a pilot.

On March 17, 1937, Amelia Earhart and Fred Noonan left California for a westward flight around the world. To start the trip, they flew their Lockheed Electra "Flying Laboratory" over the Golden Gate Bridge in California. Amelia crashed the plane while trying to take off from Hawaii, but the two survived. They would try to fly around the world again in June, but this time they would start in Miami, Florida, and head east.

# Amelia the Famous Pilot

Amelia set many records as a pilot. She was the first woman to fly at 14,000 feet. She did this in 1922. It was hard for her plane to fly that high, and the engine almost stopped many times. This must have been scary, but Amelia kept flying higher. She knew she could do it.

In 1928, Amelia flew across the Atlantic Ocean. Charles Lindbergh was the first man to fly across it alone. Amelia was the first woman to fly across it as a passenger. She flew with two men in a plane called the *Friendship*. When she returned, she wrote a book about her trip.

With other women pilots, Amelia helped start an organization called the Ninety-Nines. In 1929, they organized the Los Angeles–to–

Amelia Earhart flew many different planes during her lifetime, including her biplane (BY-playn), *Friendship*. A biplane has two wings, usually with one wing right above the other.

Cleveland Women's Air Derby. Twenty women pilots entered the eight-day race. Will Rogers, an entertainer, called it the Powder Puff Derby. The event brought more attention to women flyers.

Amelia did not want to get married, because married women could not have careers. That's just how it was in the early

Amelia married George Palmer Putnam in 1931. He published Amelia's books, and he managed her career. He connected Amelia and Amy Guest, a wealthy woman from London who paid for Amelia's trip across the Atlantic. Putnam, who was an adventurer like Amelia, explored the Arctic in 1926 and 1927. In 1939, he wrote *Soaring Wings,* a book about Amelia's life.

1900s. Then George Putnam, her manager, fell in love with her. He asked her to marry him. She said no many times. Finally she said yes, and they were married on February 7, 1931. George wanted her to keep flying and follow her dreams. They were very happy together.

Amelia wanted to fly across the Atlantic Ocean again, but this time she wanted to fly alone. George thought this was a great idea.

Amelia stands with Mayor Jimmy Walker on the steps of City Hall in New York as she receives an award in 1932. She was given the Medal of the City of New York to honor her solo flight across the Atlantic Ocean.

Amelia left on May 20, 1932. It was probably scary flying over the ocean all by herself. If something went wrong, no one could help her. But Amelia was brave. She knew she could do anything. She landed in Ireland the next day.

After this trip, Amelia was famous. She rode in parades and went to parties. She was given awards from many countries. She was the first woman to earn some of these awards.

Amelia kept flying. She made three important flights in 1935. She flew alone from Hawaii to California. She flew alone from Los Angeles to Mexico City. And she flew alone from Mexico City to New Jersey. She was the first person ever to do these things.

21

Amelia Earhart and Fred Noonan (right) prepare for their round-the-world journey. Fred once said of Amelia: "Amelia is a grand person for such a trip. She is the only woman flyer I would care to make such an expedition with. Because in addition to being a fine companion and pilot, she can take hardship as well as a man—and work like one."

# What Happened to Amelia?

Amelia didn't get tired of flying. There were many places she wanted to go.

In 1937, she decided to fly around the world. Other people had already done this, but no one had flown around the **equator** (ee-KWAY-ter). This is the biggest part of the earth, and it would take longer to fly around it. Amelia wanted to be the first person to do this.

Amelia left Oakland, California, on March 17, 1937. This time she flew with a **navigator** (NAA-vih-gay-tur). His name was Fred Noonan. He read maps while she flew the plane.

The two flew west to Hawaii. They planned to go from there to Howland Island. When

Amelia was a responsible pilot. She checked to make sure that all the equipment in her plane was working.

Amelia tried to take off from Hawaii, she wrecked the plane. After the plane was repaired, she and Noonan tried again. On June 1, 1937, they took off from Miami, Florida. This time they would fly east around the world.

The flight was scary at times. They flew through windstorms and rain. They flew over jungles and oceans. Finally they made it to Lae on New Guinea (GIH-nee), a country in the Pacific (puh-SIH-fik) Ocean. They had already flown 22,000 miles. They were almost home.

Amelia and Fred made two attempts to fly around the world. In March 1937, they flew from Oakland, California, to Hawaii, where Amelia crashed the plane during takeoff. Once the plane was repaired, they took a test flight from Oakland to Miami, Florida. They encountered many problems on the way, but they were finally ready to make an official start from Miami on June 1. This time they flew east. They made it all the way to New Guinea, then disappeared. Most people believe their plane went down somewhere in the Pacific Ocean near Howland Island.

The Pacific Ocean has thousands of small islands. Amelia and Fred planned to fly to Howland Island from Lae, New Guinea.

The last part of their trip was the most dangerous. Their next stop was tiny Howland Island. It was only two miles long and a half mile wide. It would be very hard to see this place from an airplane. The island was also 2,000 miles away from New Guinea. Amelia had to find it in time or she would run out of fuel. Yet Amelia wasn't worried. An American ship was near Howland Island. She could call them on her radio if she needed help.

Amelia and Fred left for Howland Island on July 2, 1937. She tried to call the ship a few times. The sailors could not hear her very well. Something was wrong with the radio. Her voice was fuzzy. Soon they could not hear her at all.

The last time anyone talked to Amelia Earhart was on July 3, 1937. No one knows what happened to her or to Fred. Some people think they crashed into the ocean. Others think they landed on another island and died without food. Some people even think they were taken prisoners by the Japanese (jaa-puh-NEES). In 1937, the United States and Japan were enemies. Maybe the Japanese thought Amelia and Fred were spies.

What happened to Amelia isn't as important as how she lived. She was a brave woman who was willing to try things that no one else had ever done. She made it easier for other women to be pilots. She still helps people everywhere see that they can follow their dreams, too.

Amelia Earhart statue in North Hollywood, California

# CHRONOLOGY

| | |
|---|---|
| 1897 | Amelia Earhart is born on July 24 in Atchison, Kansas. |
| 1907 | She sees first airplane at the Iowa State Fair. |
| 1915 | She graduates from Hyde Park High School in Chicago, Illinois. |
| 1916 | She studies at the Ogontz School in Philadelphia, Pennsylvania. |
| 1918 | She works as a nurse for the Red Cross in Toronto, Canada. |
| 1919 | She enrolls at Columbia University in New York City to study medicine. |
| 1920 | She moves to Los Angeles, California, sees first air show, and takes first airplane flight. |
| 1921 | She works as a clerk at a telephone company to pay for flying lessons with Neta Snook, and buys her first airplane, named *Canary*. |
| 1922 | Amelia earns her pilot's license from Federation Aeronautique Internationale; she sets women's altitude record of 14,000 feet on October 22. |
| 1926 | She works at the Denison House in Boston as a social worker. |
| 1928 | She becomes first woman to fly as a passenger across the Atlantic Ocean, and publishes her first book, titled *20 Hrs. 40 Min.* She becomes the first woman to complete a flight across the United States. She works as aviation editor for *Cosmopolitan* magazine. |
| 1929 | She becomes vice president of a commercial airline, Ludington Lines, and helps start first women pilot's organization, the Ninety-Nines. |
| 1930 | She sets women's speed record of 181 miles per hour. |
| 1931 | She marries George Palmer Putnam on February 7; sets an altitude record in an autogiro. |
| 1932 | Her second book, *The Fun of It,* is published. She becomes the first woman to fly alone across the Atlantic on May 20; becomes first woman to receive the Distinguished Flying Cross; is first woman to receive the National Geographic Society gold medal. |
| 1934 | Amelia designs clothing for her own fashion line. |
| 1935 | She becomes the first person to fly solo from Honolulu to California; Los Angeles, California, to Mexico City; and Mexico City to Newark, New Jersey. |
| 1936 | She becomes a faculty member at Purdue University. |
| 1937 | She tries to fly around the world in a Lockheed Electra. She and navigator Fred Noonan do not complete the flight. They are last heard from on July 3. |

# TIMELINE IN HISTORY

| 1485 | Leonardo da Vinci begins designing flying machines and a parachute. |
|------|---------------------------------------------------------------------|
| 1785 | John Jeffries and Jean-Pierre Blanchard fly across the English Channel in a balloon. |
| 1901 | Brazilian aviator Alberto Santos-Dumont flies around the Eiffel Tower in an airship. |
| 1903 | Orville and Wilbur Wright fly their airplane in Kitty Hawk, North Carolina. This is the first time a flying machine that is heavier-than-air takes flight. |
| 1909 | French aviator Louis Blériot becomes the first person to fly an airplane across the English Channel. |
| 1914 | World War I begins; it will last until 1917. |
| 1920 | Nineteenth Amendment to the Constitution is passed, giving women the right to vote. |
| 1927 | Charles A. Lindbergh makes a solo, nonstop flight across the Atlantic. He becomes the first person ever to do this. |
| 1929 | Stock market crashes, beginning the Great Depression. |
| 1941 | Japanese bomb Pearl Harbor in Hawaii. The U.S. enters World War II—a war that will last until 1945. |
| 1947 | U.S. pilot Charles E. Yeager flies faster than the speed of sound in a Bell X-1 airplane. |
| 1950 | Korean War begins; it will end in 1953. |
| 1957 | The Soviet Union launches *Sputnik 1*, the first human-made satellite to orbit Earth. |
| 1959 | Vietnam War begins; it will last until 1975. |
| 1961 | The Soviet Union sends their first cosmonaut, Yuri Gagarin, into space. |
| 1962 | John H. Glenn Jr. becomes the first American to orbit Earth. |
| 1969 | The United States land men on the moon. Neil A. Armstrong and Edwin E. Aldrin Jr. become the first men to walk on the moon. |
| 1971 | The Soviet Union builds the first space station. |
| 1981 | The United States launches its first space shuttle, the *Columbia*, into space. This is the first reusable spacecraft to orbit Earth. |
| 1998 | The International Space Station is launched into space. |
| 2000 | The first crew to live on the International Space Station is launched into space. |
| 2004 | The United States' Mars Rover lands on Mars. |
| 2007 | Record-setting aviator Steven Fossett is lost when his plane goes down in western Nevada. |

# FIND OUT MORE

## Books

Bull, Angela. *DK Readers: Flying Ace, The Story of Amelia Earhart.* New York: DK Publishing, 2000.

DeVillier, Christy. *Amelia Earhart.* Edina, Minnesota: Ado Consulting Group, 2001.

Jerome, Kate Boehm. *Who Was Amelia Earhart?* New York: Grosset and Dunlap, 2002.

Lakin, Patricia. *Amelia Earhart: More Than a Flier.* New York: Aladdin Paperbacks, 2003.

Sutcliffe, Jane. *Amelia Earhart.* Minneapolis, Minnesota: Lerner Publications Company, 2003.

Wheeler, Jill C. *Amelia Earhart.* Edina, Minnesota: Ado Consulting Group, 2002.

## Works Consulted

Butler, Susan. *East to the Dawn: The Life of Amelia Earhart.* Reading, Massachusetts: Addison-Wesley, 1997.

Earhart, Amelia. *20 Hrs. 40 Min.: Our Flight in the* Friendship. New York: Putnam, 1928.

Earhart, Amelia. *The Fun of It: Random Records of My Own Flying and of Women in Aviation.* New York: Brewer, Warren & Putnam, 1932.

Earhart, Amelia. *Last Flight.* New York: Harcourt, Brace, and Company, 1937.

King, Thomas F. *Amelia Earhart's Shoes: Is the Mystery Solved?* Walnut Creek, California: AltaMira Press, 2001.

"Miss Earhart Off on Pacific Flight." *New York Times,* January 11, 1935.

Putnam, George Palmer. *Soaring Wings.* New York: Harcourt, Brace and Company, 1939.

Raymond, Allen. "Amelia Earhart Flies Atlantic, First Woman to Do It." *New York Times,* June 17, 1928.

**On the Internet**

Amelia Earhart Birthplace Museum
  http://www.ameliaearhartmuseum.org

National Air and Space Museum: *Pioneers of Flight Gallery.*
  "Lockheed 5 Vega" http://www.nasm.si.edu/research/aero/
  aircraft/lockheed_5b.htm

The Official Site of Amelia Earhart http://www.ameliaearhart.com

Purdue University Libraries Archives and Special Collections: *George
  Palmer Putnam Collection of Amelia Earhart Papers.* "Amelia
  Earhart Biographical Sketch" http://www.lib.purdue.edu/spcol/
  aearhart/index.html

U.S. Centennial of Flight Commission: *Explorers, Daredevils, and
  Record Setters,* "Amelia Earhart"
  http://www.centennialofflight.gov/essay/
  Explorers_Record_Setters_and_Daredevils/earhart/EX29.htm

# GLOSSARY

altitude (AL-tih-tood)—Height above level ground or the sea.

career (kuh-REER)—The type of job a person is trained to do and
  does for a long time.

canary (kuh-NAIR-ee)—A small yellow bird.

college (KAH-lidj)—A school of higher learning that a person goes to
  after high school.

equator (ee-KWAY-ter)—The imaginary circle around the earth that is
  halfway between the North and South Poles.

navigator (NAA-vih-gay-tur)—A person who is in charge of an
  airplane's course of direction.

taxied (TAK-seed)—Drove a plane along the ground.

# INDEX

249 2946

JB          Leavitt, Amie Jane
EARHART     What's So Great About
            Amelia Earhart?

$15.95